MOON OVER ZABRISKIE

Thanks to the poets of Sixteen Rivers Press; Murray Silverstein, Gillian Wegener, Lynne Knight, Jerry Fleming, Carolyn Miller; the Whitmaniacs' writing group & David St. John; Richard Silberg & Joyce Jenkins of Poetry Flash, Edward Smallfield, Mark Doty, Amy Gerstler, Ed Ochester, Eve Pell, Jane Hirshfield, Babette Jenny, Marguerite Cunningham, Pina Piccolo, my brothers, Michael and Timothy Wickes; and Don Stang

Moon Over Zabriskie
Copyright © 2014 Helen Wickes
Paperback ISBN: 978-0-9840352-4-3

All rights reserved: except for the purpose of quoting brief passages for review, no part of this book may be reproduced or transmitted in any form or by any means, electronic or mechanical, including photocopying, recording, or by any information storage and retrieval system, without permission in writing from the publisher.

Cover art: Michael Wickes
Cover design: Steven Asmussen
Design & Layout: Steven Asmussen

Glass Lyre Press, LLC.
P.O. Box 2693
Glenview, IL 60026

www.GlassLyrePress.com

MOON OVER ZABRISKIE

Poems by
Helen Wickes

Praise for *Moon Over Zabriskie*

Helen Wickes' new collection of poems, Moon over Zabriskie, is a rare combination: deeply grounded in the deepest layers of Earth, yet radiant in its mystical understanding of souls traversing the "hour of reinvention before sunrise." A keen observer of the ephemeral events of life, both beautiful and spawning "marrow-deep grief," Wickes shines like "Orion on his side over Zabriskie Point."

Karen Bowles, Publisher of *Luciole Press*

"I don't know where Zabriskie is, or the Funeral Mountains or Titus Canyon or Furnace Creek. I've never been the places Helen Wickes has been or seen the things she has. But her easy-flowing narratives, luscious imagery, organic even seemingly effortless reflections and association transport me to other places and times that miraculously feel importantly familiar. What else could one hope for from poetry?"

Scott Owens, Author of
For One Who Knows How to Own Land

For Don

Acknowledgements

Arroyo Literary Review: "Serenade for the Gold Country," "Late Night Stroll in the Valley"

Bryant Literary Review: "Orange Poppies"

CALYX Journal: "Pilgrimage up Henderson Canyon Road," "Rabbits Keep My Father Alive"

Chicago Quarterly Review: "Day after Easter, Point Reyes"

Corium Magazine: "The Heart Waking up Braids Her Hair"

Delmarva Review: "Jacob and the Angel," "Caravaggio's The Incredulity of St. Thomas," "Caravaggio's The Conversion of St. Paul," "Caravaggio's Burial of Santa Lucia"

Euphony: "What You Can Hear"

Evansville Review: "Orange Poppies," "The Moon over Zabriskie"

FRIGG: A Magazine of Fiction and Poetry: "Nude Barbie Dines at Stellina's"

Jabberwock Review: "We Are Only Temporary Custodians of Beauty"

Journal: "November Chill and All the Animals"

Minetta Review: "Frost, Then Ice," "The Heart Waking up Braids Her Hair"

Natural Bridge: "Drinking the Blue"

Picayune Literary Magazine: "Palm Canyon"

Poet Lore: "Silver Lake Rituals"

SLAB: "Rabbits Keep My Father Alive"

Softblow: "Cebolla, New Mexico," "Elements of Style," "What You Hope For," "Not a Georgia O'Keeffe in Sight"

South Dakota Review: "Titus Canyon"

Southwest American Literature: "Gold Canyon"

Splash of Red: "Frost, Then Ice," "Sense of Direction"

The Louisville Review: "Pilgrimage up Henderson Canyon"

Tower Journal: "Watershed," "Occultation," "Another Saturday Night," "Solstice Freeze"

Whisperings: "Borrego Springs," "If the Desert Acts Familiar, Push Back," "Palm Canyon"

Words and Images: "Blue Jay Morning"

Contents

Barn on Fire

Pilgrimage Up Henderson Canyon Road	19
We Are Only Temporary Custodians of Beauty	21
Barn on Fire	23
Orange Poppies	25
Day After Easter, Point Reyes	27
A Small Prayer in Small Stitches	28
Ode to My Mother	30
Rabbits Keep My Father Alive	32
What You Can Hear	34

Drinking the Blue

Surface of Winter	39
Drinking the Blue	40
The Heart Waking Up Braids Her Hair	42
Nude Barbie Dines at Stellina's	44
Frost, Then Ice	45
Cebolla, New Mexico	47
Not a Georgia O'Keeffe in Sight	49
Elements of Style	51
Serenade for the Gold Country	53

Watershed

What You Hope For	56
Still Life With Hoof Prints	58
Jacob and the Angel	59
Caravaggio's *The Incredulity of St. Thomas*	61
Caravaggio's *On the Conversion of St. Paul*	63
Caravaggio's *Burial of Santa Lucia*	64
Occultation	66

Another Saturday Night 67
Solstice Freeze 69
Watershed 70

Moon Over Zabriskie

Sense of Direction 74
Silver Lake Rituals 75
Blue Jay Morning 76
Borrego Springs 77
If The Desert Acts Familiar, Push Back 78
The Yellow Sand Road 79
Palm Canyon 81
Gold Canyon 83
Moon Over Zabriskie 85
Furnace Creek Breakdown 87
Titus Canyon 88
Autumn Ballad 89
Late Night Stroll in the Valley 91

BARN ON FIRE

I

Pilgrimage Up Henderson Canyon Road

Pilgramage up Henderson Canyon Road

I once was on intimate terms
with an entire grapefruit orchard,

and each February, for years, drove out to smell
the perfume of Seley Reds in bloom.

Everyone wants solace for their marrow-deep grief,

and oh, how we cast our nets of desire
over a place and beg for it to flourish, even

in our absence: a small room, a café, that bad dirt road,
with rabbits in the headlights.

No sir, I said, *didn't come out to steal your fruit*

(who would drive to the edge of nowhere
for grapefruit at midnight?) *I've come for the air,*

smelling of white flowers, fertilizer, and dust.

That was then. My trees, my easy ticket
to temporary Heaven, now past their prime
at 30 years, are all cut down.

The dead ones, a mountain of twisted wood.

The rows of spindly baby trees are sipping
from their drip lines,

the half-moon above, and one moth in a tizzy.

Don't go lecturing me about *attachment
and brevity*. If I fail

and fail again to describe the scent,
try to remember the voice of someone

years after they have died, the lingering sound.

How you become whatever clings to you,
what dies into you.

We Are Only Temporary Custodians of Beauty

Don't you sometimes want to lie down
and look up at the birds?

Specifically, the white pelicans migrating this month,
the unrepeatable patterns
they make and unmake as they hold the sky in place.

*

After a long wait alone on the telephone, I finally said,
*How dare you
put me on hold this long*

to the absolutely no one there, to no one
on the other end.

*

That night someone tried to steal my car
with scissors and left a broken blade

in the door, another broken blade
in the ignition. The tow truck guy number one

hiccups and reeks of booze. *Angel,*
he says, *get a gun,*

but tow truck guy number two, snaggletoothed,
with tattooed dragons
and bleeding hearts, says, *Lady, get a dog.*

I think back to Chekhov's lady and her dog
and tried to remember its color, yes, was white.

The men argue about guns and dogs and grenades.
Snaggletooth says,
Get yourself a decent car.

                             *

Above me: finch, tree, nest, springtime.

Wouldn't you love to drive out to the country,
to find that roving flock of white pelicans,

and rest beneath them for a solid hour?

Barn on Fire

I'm the witch in cheap satin; my brother's
the red devil. Our friends: a Frankenstein,
several ghosts, a green-goggled Martian.
We've only toyed with the infernal.

Here's the real thing. Flames batter
the night sky. There's the bitter taste of ash,
the smother of heat, the fiery blaze. Our great barn
burning. We stare into it.

We'd left our mother and father alone
to pull 11 horses to safety from their stalls
while we were out gallivanting
in our pretend infernal drag. Above the barn
a ton of tight-baled clover hay and golden straw
waiting to explode were fuel for this.

The stories swirl: a madman, a drunk,
a match, bad wires, bad luck. The reporter
calls our parents heroes, while we children fret
about the horses: fat Blue Bell, sweet Tiger,
huge Jack. Where will we house them?
A guy from town arranges us on the fire truck
and shoves a camera in our faces. Can't catch
the main thing: how we won't ever count
on the beloved, any beloved, to stay put.
Ladybug, ladybug, your house is on fire.
If it is there when we get home,
grace intervened.

My brother and I will carry on,
not always with joy, not always
with dread, and, like you, perhaps

we will find clean-hand city work;
we will become, like you, absorbed
into the many, out there
among the passersby.

Orange Poppies

They do their best to deceive you,
the satiny sheen of their petals
fluttering on skinny, leek-green stalks,
odorless as a gas leak.
Each spring I bring a wild one home,
watch it from across the room
until its petals wither, plop off
one by one. Its color floats back
to the hell it came from.

Orange is the color of madness.
Not the dark, slow, bury-me-alive kind,
not the bright, loud, I'll-buy-ten-charge-
them-to-the-gods kind.
See for yourself; orange poppies,
mockeries of real flowers,
lounge in the field by drifts of blue:
larkspur, lupine—
blue's the color of thought,
of windows thrown open.
Orange poppies are unchosen thoughts.

Try to approach blue lupine.
Poppies, burning with jealousy,
glowing with envy,
won't let you.
Lower your face to them.
No one will pull you.
Poppies aren't a doorway plant—
no transport, no trance.

By June they look dead. But do not relax.
The glossy, black seeds in dry husks
quietly plump themselves all summer.
They are patient; they will return.

Day After Easter, Point Reyes

How stupidly resolute the body that carries all our anger—
        the heft of lead, potency of mercury— there once was
an angel of anger, but she shook herself free. How frail

our breath as it spends and spends itself into what?
Though this hillside's far too steep to look at without feeling ill,
huge rocks hold it in place with rose-bellied clouds

keeping a lid on us all. Who's out there, can you hear?
Thanks for solitude crowding me down into the daffodil's
lemony scent, sorrow's true flowers, a whole swath of them

by the boulders. How trustworthy they seem, these rocks
        and blossoms, pleasures of time. Under the breeze-
blown green, pale roots, and deeper, the white bones

        not crumbled. But for once, be still,
you sliding days, you imperious hours, you're silt
between my fingers. I fling you back.

A Small Prayer in Small Stitches

That in the eyes of the Maker
we will thirst no more, that's one

slender-hinged reverie snapped shut
from the brouhaha over there:

the too green and the golf course skulkers,
plumply pastelled, thwacking

and ruminative. The ball teeters
as my tongue edges the drop-off

from where my own tooth was recently
yanked. A distant golfer stares prayerfully.

Vacationing in the dark
heat of a nostalgic impulse,

said Orson Welles, who knew
how from out of the green sward,

these blues. And so I'm settled
to mad scribbling about the fir trees,
whose pointy tips scratch the fog's belly,

and how elsewhere California's
sun shines generally, steeping
the inner land, blasting the snowy,

basting to a slow roil
the salted edges. A mother's voice

forever ago, cloven tongue

of fire, an imbroglio, speaking
through sluiced streams—
go sleep in your solitude,

tonight, the night after. O Lord,
*make me kind, but keep me
a little ruthless.*

Ode to My Mother

How silly it often looked to us,
all that living she jammed into her days,
those final years. Spray painting pinecones gold,

stenciling blue tulips onto wooden boxes, running
the pink hollyhocks up every wall, while we,
the indolent ones—
amazed, amused—looked on and rolled our eyes.

Her dozen wind chimes
haunted our nights. She weeded
and mowed. The rains came, then the sun, the fields

needed mowing again. She pampered the weanlings,
named the yearlings, fretted about the mares,
bought oils and brushes and canvas,
books on perspective, new hats for occasions,

new collars for the cats. Her frantic joy
and her smiting rage every hour swapped partners
and danced, the music

got louder and faster, even the sunlight felt dizzy
to us. She accounted for every second
of her life, perfected each inch of each acre. As if her soul
were about to tip the scale. But remember,

we'd tell one another, *this was
her own homemade Eden,*
and she its only God, Scourge, Whirlwind, Shout

from the Garden. Please note the forest of baskets
dangling from the rafters, the walnuts gilded golden

for Christmas. For years we spied,
hoping to catch her

staring at dust motes. Wanted to find her
mumbling to ghosts or even slack-handed,
scribbling on a page. Wanted to find her.

Rabbits Keep My Father Alive

There were four: piebald, white,
a dun, one black. They have
multiplied. He leaves them loose,
builds tunnels and lean-tos
against tree trunks for shade,
escape doors to the tractor shed,
sets down saucers of water.

He warns them about owls and foxes
but won't cage them. Never tries
to touch them. All he offers them—
is companionship and snacks.
No protection.

The summer evenings sneak up on him.
He snaps and tosses carrots.
His rabbits emerge shyly
and eat in full view.

They rise and sniff,
the males slam the ground
with their hind legs. The youngsters careening.
They have black currant eyes.
He talks to them about dead friends,
favorite dogs who died,
his strange, aging children,
his very busy, busy wife.

He tells his rabbits about landing
at Anzio, the sound of bombs,
faces of the unsaved, the ship
home from Naples. Flinging carrots,
he stumbles through scraps of Italian,
those arias he used to sing.

He often imagines his own body
covered in rabbits' fur.
It lets him approach
the brevity of their lives.

What You Can Hear

The whir of the planet pulled into dusk—
if I hold up the phone, can you hear it?
And did you catch the snapping shut
of the swallows' wing tip feathers, the plop
of the spider laying eggs in the nest,
clouds' resistance to being ripped in two,
and the moonlight's plink on my windowpane,
sound that the soul makes—a click or an ooh—
slipping into, then out of the body it chooses,
and now serotonin, that bright sizzle,
cut loose in the synapse, after the purr
of recognition soothing the amygdala:
a person, a human face, appears at my door,
are you still listening?

Are you still listening?
A person, a human face, appears at my door;
recognition soothes the amygdala
with a purr, and now, in the synapse,
serotonin, that bright sizzle, is cut loose,
then the click or the ooh, sound the soul makes
slipping in, then out of the body it chooses,
the plink of moonlight on my windowpane,
and clouds' resistance to being torn in two,
and the plop of the eggs laid by the spider
in the nest, and did you catch the way
the swallows' wing tip feathers snap shut?
And if I hold up this phone, can you hear it,
the whir of the planet pulled into dusk?

DRINKING THE BLUE

II

Surface of Winter

Between the rain's onslaught and downpour,
the sun in blazes slips a foot through the door,
the blossoms of the Michelia flaring
into white, the fuchsia running a pink riot
up the wall. The whole garden

gone crazy green, wet-lit in a deep-drawn breath
of green in reprieve, mournful and ecstatic,
like Cezanne's shadowless green,
praised by Rilke in a lonely letter home,
in which he wrote about how colors

should be set loose upon the canvas
to sort themselves out,
which is what they're doing outside,
this herd of colors, snorting and sniffing
and squealing, choosing sides,
wondering who's in charge.

Down the street, an engine stalls, horn blares,
doors slam, then the usual screaming voices
in a *lingua franca* uproar. In the late light,
a soaked raccoon tests the crosswalk,
some invisible protector
nudging him home.

Out back, the Meyer lemon languishes,
in a yellow-leafed sulk,
fortunate tree with your nameable, fixable hunger.

Drinking the Blue

Because the hills turn their backs on sunlight,
the whole landscape rolling out from under,
you see that light is the lover,
never the beloved, and wonder whether day has gone

into waste or grist.
The next-door twins are selling lemonade,
quarter a shot, asking, Is it any good?
The answer being, very sour, and they say,

parents don't like sugar. Not a parent, I tell them
I can live on sweets, a sentence they enjoy,
but this lemonade they're selling is blue-green,

color of something you'd flush drains with,
oxide of tin or copper, an acidic, cerulean blue,
promising an aftertaste like a memory
of a not-great pleasure,
now sorely grieved

only because it was once urgently desired.
Something that could have been sold downstream
for beads and firewood.
With sugar, the lemonade swirls into the sky color
of a Giotto fresco,

above the bead-praying monks, behind the cypress,
before the earthquake, before the rubble,
before the frantic search for: Here, this red tile
a fragment of tunic, this one—of skin—now here's

an eyebrow. This hunger to piece human countenance
out of the dust. These kids are transfixed,
as if they could see the blue pour down my throat,

staining my body from inside out,
as if they hope for alchemical change. In the sky's alembic
the summer solstice pulls us toward dusk.

The Heart Waking Up Braids Her Hair

But I digress, which is where I found you
In a glass house gathering no moss
With the scent of lemons, sound of two flutes
Remotely controlled and fully erasable

A glass house which gathers no moss
Please sit still and I'll tell you
It's remotely controlled, fully erasable
The language taking aim at the soundless

Sit still, I'm telling you the story
A repertoire of sound spilled at your feet
Language taking aim at the soundless
It doesn't matter if you packed the right clothes

A repertoire of tricks poured over your feet
Phobia supplants epiphany, then wants a kiss
It doesn't matter if you lack the right clothes
Astound me with your voice, all suede, ice cube,

Phobia supplanting epiphany, wanting that kiss
A field we hoped would contain us
Surround me with your voice: violets, ice cubes
Mad for the blue and you as you are meant to be

In the field we were sure would contain us
Until the bright comes forward, shows its face
Mad for the blue of what's enough, what's next
Again the question, as you are meant to believe

Until the bright comes toward you, shows its face
Shows the scent of lemons, sound of two flutes
Shows the question, what's enough, what's next
But I digress, which is where I found you.

Nude Barbie Dines at Stellina's

At least eleven of them settle in,
      the small girl's got a Barbie naked,
save for underpants and red hair, luxuriant and streaming
      to the little arched toes. The kid

wraps the hair around the pointy breasts,
between the rigid legs, eagerly locating
      new places. The mother fidgets, the father
queries the wine list. They order up oysters, splash them
with lemon, and salt, Tabasco,
lustily slurping the brine.

A bored brother grabs and twists the doll's legs
      behind its tiny ears, other brother snatches it,
wrapping its body with its voluptuous hair. Later, dessert,
brandies. Much yelling, an uncle

storms out, a teen films everything on her phone,
      another madly texting. Grandma snatches the doll
from an aunt, turns its face to the table, jumps it—
      her?—up and down, whole family

hollering—sorry I don't know their language—the mother,
sullen all evening, snatches the awful doll,
      mummifies it in her napkin, hurls it at grandfather,
and just when you think—*oh families, such joy, now mom*

will rush away sobbing, but no, she arises very slowly
stares at each of us, one by one, straight in the eye,
      and blank-faced, glides very slowly
out of the room, the building, into the evening.

Frost, Then Ice

The coyotes' dawn sound—
ice fragments chipping the air.
Sprinkle of stars, white on the mountains.
Rain stings the tin roof at night.
Lightning glaring into this window, into the next.

All day the wind roars in from Chama.
The big-bodied crows flail
and take to their fence posts,
the vast meadows shove the mountains back.

In this one acre there's a still place,
where you can't hear trucks
grind uphill toward Colorado,
or that distressed, bawling sound of cattle,
as if they knew their fate;

but you can hear small things: water in the creek,
the wings of a raptor who scours the ground.
He tilts, I should know his name, my mind's vague.

In the Cebolla graveyard
five iron bedsteads guard the few graves.
Here lies, rest in peace, cribs for the babies.
When the Spanish came, this valley smelled
of wild onions. Today it smells of snow.

My bird's a marsh hawk, he owns this meadow,
a diurnal flesh eater, the books say,
takes prey live. Behind me the empty hammock

lashed from elm to porch, thrashes in the wind,
colors bled, strings sprung, a sad thing.
Someone should climb in, anchor it down.

Today the whole world is thin ice and we're skating,
giddy with speed,
swerving the rough places,
always about to turn for home,
which is farther than we thought.

Cebolla, New Mexico

Raked sky, slurred clouds,
the dirt road to town is a center part
through the rye grass,
and on the chamisa, a breath of ice.

A retired Santa Fe boxcar hunkers in the field,
housing the wares of the purveyor
of Victorian undergarments. Her wares
a still life in satin and velvet,
chamois, and bengaline, hand-crafted

exoskeletons from thorax to belly,
defying the logistics of bosom and breath,
worn inside out when the stays wear down.
Bustles cost more, they stop the eye,

as do those billboards of bandoleros,
crisscrossed with cartridge belts,
outside Tierra Amarilla,
saying land or death, land or death.

I pace the fence line
and throw one rock at another for the sound.
The people here were too loud all day
and have gone to Chama for lunch.
I sent them away, now want them home.

I ponder the lacing of a corset,
which requires an extra pair of hands,
and how signature markings

along a woman's naked back can be read,
revealing just who has left
his runic imprint upon her skin.

I often wonder what the mind wants for the body,
this cash crop, this risen dough.
There are many ways to bind the living.
So much keeps breaking out: the mountains
through the metallic, ambered light,

the day, which seems eager to be lived.
I could nearly give in to it,
to the cold that burns cottonwoods into color,
to the insistent sound of an engine changing gears.

Not a Georgia O'Keeffe in Sight

Evening rises from the canyon floor.
Colder by the minute,
songbirds sing louder, pickups growl uphill.
Frost has burst the pinyon cones,
sticky, fragrant, thick with seeds.

For a week in Albuquerque
people dangle from gaudy balloons,
tethered to earth by radio.
They tangle in phone wires,
obsessed with ballast and gravity.

Stones clatter, two boys in the arroyo
scramble for the lion-colored Siamese cat.
A man calls them home for dinner,
right now, this instant, do you hear me.

I have here an ad from the Neptune Society,
one seagull and a message,
Leave with dignity and still afford it.
If birds carry the soul to Heaven,
who decided it should be a seagull?

Bonnard saying he used objects
as a source of intimidation,
as good a wisdom as a body needs tonight.
Find your object. Keep it scary.
Anything will do,

this sheet of paper, glitter-eyed birds,
or the juniper-handled light through the window
sliding across the bed,
soft-knit butter light,
enough to grab hold of,
roll around in, plenty left for winter.

Elements of Style

Waking to fog, the fog declining its chance
to unfasten pearl buttons from its wrist
and shake hands with the blue. On the ledge
a green parrot sings his one song,

mimics the sound of electronic warfare
pouring from a video arcade.
To achieve clarity, they say: *be clear,*
be concrete, avoid the passive,

and save emphatic language for the end.
At the end of my street, newspapers in racks,
many choices and such a modest vice. Give in
and there goes the morning's poem,

take your pick. Jingle your pocket change,
glance at headlines while pretending not to,
then look away, remembering the woman
at the South Pole,

needing to cut into her own breast,
to figure things out alone and fix them.
The end of her story, so far, unknown.

The paper is bought. Getting from the real
to the imagined space is immense and delicate.
In the supermarket line the blind woman
says she can crack her eggs

for a soufflé, *keeping her yolks from her whites
by feel*, making me think of that saint
breaking open a honeycomb,
all that trapped light spilling out, flying back

into space. Next to us in line,
50-pound child flaunting her dismay,
someone else muttering about *a muzzle
and leash*. They say, as a writer, you must *remain

in the background; don't be breezy and don't explain.*

Serenade for the Gold Country

Caterpillars crochet a white shroud
over a sapling. All day things fall.
Bark from Plane Trees,
green pears that won't ripen.

I'm off to Arnie's Blue Bird café for chips,
to the room to lie on the bed,
to watch the slow ceiling fan.

By noon the sky squeezes down,
the day a grape in the gods' winepress,
the last sip of life pressed out.

From my window this Victorian town
and underneath it a boarded-up world,
honeycomb of tunnels and shafts,
capillaries of abandoned gold mines.

Imagine the miners
and their blindfolded mules,
ratcheted a mile down to carve the matrix,
then hoisted at the day's end into glare and smell.

Finally, the storm arrives, all call and response,
thunder hollering at the white, flung-out
sheets of lightning.

When rain comes it's tropical, great fat drops
of exuberant diva rain. And then the air floods back
into town, rolling off the mountains
and lifting up the skirts of the trees.

form
WATERSHED

III

What You Hope For

The day trying its best to heat up,
the snow breathing cool off the mountains
in July. As the amber iris fades,
the golden mule ears open—it's a yellow translation.

In the forest there are thrown-out tires,
a splayed-open fridge, old windows.
The moss on the trees is too bright,
a hot, green tangle. It's hard to get away,
but from what, toward what?

A mashed place
in the rye grass where the deer sleep.
And then I find a tiny bird's nest imprinted inside
by underbelly, heartbeat, but the outer twigs
roughed up by onslaught.

The loud camper passes, loaded down
with bikes and rowboat, dragging a jeep.
People together—an act of courage,
how they do this.

The beauty bounces off the surface,
the morning strokes the mist from the lake.
The day's thin-skinned but not for long.

On the lake one canoe swerves,
then lurches. How worrisome
to watch the two people, cosseted
in their bosomy life jackets, jerkily stand up

and exchange words, exchange paddles.
Their bouncing boat soon rights itself. Ah well,
crying is not an option.
You can get love wrong again
and become an expert of the aftermath.

The climbing body thinks: *left foot,
mariposa lily, right foot, three stones;*
three stones means a trail,
another person's been here before us.

This high up there's heat, granite,
and silence. A steady drizzle of pebbles
skittering down the slope.

Still Life With Hoof Prints

The wind thrashing the elm, smoky from a fire
in the valley. *Beware of mothering
the death of beauty*, says the planet Venus,
glowering at dawn, morning star in a sea of ink.

Scroll me a line, I'll take dictation
in this hour of reinvention before sunrise.

Morning's first word misspells itself in my mind,
I thought of *Chiton*, meaning Greek tunic in Doric
or Ionic, white linen in folds,

by midmorning my semidreamed word makes a leap
to *Chitin*, the thin-crackling armor
of insects, translucent as fine glaze.

Under the blue glaze of the sky, nothing finer
than the way eight horses stop running
and listen. Dust in whorls

and smoke along the hills. Memory slides
to the blue stain of the too-permanent words
a mother pens into shirt collars for sleepaway.

The half-dozing horse lifts his foot to receive
another shoe. The starched shirts have long gone for rags,
but the image is imprinted forever of the hand

inking letters, her hard-pressed midnight scrawl,
her hand ironing the letters onto white cotton shirts.
Somewhere the smell of ink. The smell of smoke.

Jacob and the Angel

Like dust, if on earth blowing east, the squatter evades,
then he's pleading, Ladder me up there again. And the angel,
her cold eyes not leaving the traveler's face.

If he could hold her still long enough,
but her fingers burrowing into his neck, tuning his rib cage,

she's a great thing pressing, not fully formed, though
scented, and shapely as a child's mind,
then he remembers to demand, *Not until you…*

her wings pinned back in a frown,
their breaths entangled, the way fog enters a cloud,
which she's enjoying as if it were taking place inside her.

The way oil poured on a stone makes it not a stone, but an
altar to what's to come, measured out in dreams of sheaves—

that's the beyond he's bargained for, cut open upon the rock,
that's how he's asking, *What do you want*, shoving her off
him, out of him, but lingering, against her fingers,

those sticky and feathered. Her own desires are few,
maybe she craves the occasional silken swagger of human
skin.

The sound of his shuffling and dealing, calling and bluffing.
All the while she unscrolls his future, tries to lure him
past incandescence into what's stained and more.
He won't go there, even with his white bone snapped,
his strummed sinews hold, and his small mind slides around

all that's fractured. All night, through the octaves ascending
and descending. How little he wants to know amazes her,
for whom this shoving and hissing and whispering,
bringing him nearly to pitch, then unloosening his strings,
must continue until morning and beyond.

Caravaggio's *The Incredulity of St. Thomas*

He can't mean this; he does mean this—
one hand guided by another
into the damage, the horizontal slit,
a little bloodied, slightly gaping.

On the lawn a tree discards yellow leaves,
although it's July. Half the tree in viridian,
midsummer immersion. Half's gone on ahead.

I think it's done in silence,
but how far can you press the silky surface,
the mannerist seduction, the face of this man
who's agreed to leave the known?

Thinking today is distracted by commotion
at the next table, the calling out
for a BLT, bacon crispy, hold the mayo,
extra for her, and bring a shake.

Not an easy painting to live with—
its insistence on the limb-tangled embrace
of desire and question.
How urgently they call up one another.

As children we hovered both hands
over the gas jet's blue flame
to learn how close we could get,
and our bodies still hold.
That's how Thomas gives his right hand,
dirty nails and all, to the one who's absent
or not. Our eyes flicker to the left hand,
the one clutching his red shirt,
as if asking, *What's to become of me?*

Outside, today, grapevines twine their stakes,
order subduing the rampant,
which half wants to be overrun

by ripeness with its musky smell
of fruit rubbing against fruit,
the slight surrender at skin's boundary
in the hot days before harvest and crush.

Caravaggio's *On the Conversion of St. Paul*

We don't have to like his saint,
splayed in the middle of the road,
don't have to understand the illegible
gestures made by his arms flailing in air,
this man who would, if he could, alter hearts
by telling the few they're gold, as for the rest—
we'll burn. But our painter—who has yet
to leave a man dying from a street brawl
in Rome—he cherishes epiphany's flash
more than its prelude

or wake. In this painting notice how
he's placed the horse, a sweet-faced,
unkempt skewbald, who curls around
the fallen man, one foreleg raised
so as not to injure. This artist's
borrowed dray horse, led clattering
to the upstairs studio, swerves one ear
to the background, other ear
beyond the picture frame. In his mouth

a shanked bit, likely the sort
with sharp-pronged rollers,
so that when you tug the reins
the bit will drag you
five centuries back before Saul
became Paul, all the way to Xenophon,
instructing how to train your war horse
with a bit so severe, one touch and yes,
he'll obey, but won't
love you. Hardly the point
for a soon-to-be saint
in whose tumble out of matter
toward purity, no easy conversation
between rider and ridden,
no pleasure permitted.

Caravaggio's *Burial of Santa Lucia*

The figures look quickly sketched,
as if the artist were distracted
and hurried to get it over with,
his two massive grave diggers,
his hunched-over mourners,

that dead saint sprawled on the floor,
one arm gesturing at us, her neck weirdly bent.
Is she, like his dying Mary,
modeled on some drowned whore,
just fished from the icy waters of the sea?

Outside today is a November evening,
a red-gold infusion, backlighting the elms,
Rothko light, eerily warm,

through which you could nearly reach,
to tell him, from here,
that something might work out.

Because in the postcards and the cheaper texts
they chop off half of Caravaggio's painting,
you're left with just travail
and the turmoil of grief
and can't see that vast interior space
stretching beyond the figures,
pure Baroque, slightly lit

from without and from within,
this darkened harvest of air
soaring above time's havoc—
what else is chiaroscuro?

Outside then, in Siracusa, Sicily,
it is 1608, and after rendering the saint
who traded her eyes for a soul,

the painter, who knew
that either one evokes the other,
has barely three more years to live.

The mood of this hovering, cavernous space
is late Rothko, a lit infusion of dust,
each dust mote vibrant with duration,
a dense universe of grief, arising from
and bearing down upon the human realm,
which doesn't notice.

Occultation

The moon gobbled the sun for lunch, that's
what the man from Karachi says on the radio,
talking us through midday's midnight,
telling us he's *nostalgic for the Babylonians*,

who, during their eclipses, smashed crockery
to hasten the light. *Oh, wishful humans.*
Here in this parking lot, in a tin pail
of ordinary yellow zinnia splendor,

there is one flower, solar, radial, fringed,
centripetal, which I desperately want
and which the veiled and turbaned vendor
won't sell, won't give. How to bargain

when I can't see her eyes, what's she hiding—
beauty or danger? I can't keep them straight.
Black sunflower, she calls this flower.
I'd settle for its smolder, a slow combustion

of dark red threatening to scorch,
contracting toward night and failing to do so,
the color stewing, fermenting, thick
and pungent as summer's ripening heart.

Another Saturday Night

One coyote, fat and bold,
rushing uphill, turns to look back.
Evening plays a chordal descent, a delayed backbeat,
a Sam Cooke sunset, the coyote a copper smudge
behind the manzanita and oak.

The tule fog gropes the valley,
low to the ground, as if waiting
to be pulled under, sucked back
through any roadside ditch.

The whole week gone, like a partially eaten meal
whisked away before you've placed the cutlery
at three-fifteen, to signal *I'm finished.*

Out of the plowed field,
a flock of starlings, dark sprouts
sprung forth. Buddy Holly,
notes by the mouthful,
that trick of heat and youth.

Raving on. The famous critics say
that poems now *are all anecdote with epiphany.*
They'd dislike me. Let them.
Right now I'd settle for epiphany,
with or without the anecdote.

When you can't get to the thin edge
of your own living, when you can't sharpen it
and run barefoot, it hardly seems worthwhile.

The cold sneaks in, a clingy, seacoast cold,
a joint tightener, heart toughener.
A black cat, out of nowhere,
young and greedy, jumps to my lap,
wants all of me. What's left for tonight
is subject to fits and lives on thin air.

Solstice Freeze

One angus crosses the field,
a laggard stopping to holler,
his herd gone on without him.

The short days tightening a belt
around the year's waistline. Under brown hillsides
bright green articulates the bone
of creek bed, outcrop, fire trail to the peak.

The cyclers shimmer past in nylon,
churning insects, pumping their torsos
as if they had only one life
to hoist over the hill to the reservoir.

There's the faint noise of a plane
and of a small bird through bare branches.
A hospital message said, *pray for no clots,*
your mother's heart,
syncopation, skipping beats.

The angus all one herd now,
outcast submerged, indistinguishable.
Black cream clotting, curds from whey
bottled, flung out, who will find it?

In the city I stop to watch bagpipe players
tune up in a parking lot,
twisting their drone pipes,
honking and bleating, a farmyard in kilts.

Imagine the source in a bellows
under your arm, which you unloosen
note by note until the sound
drowns out everything.

After raggedy scales the flailing
into fifths: convergence, melody.

Watershed

A black dog ferries his goat herd home,
eases the lumpy mass of them
through a narrow gate, along a narrow path,

and the goats toying with the dog,
herd animals – but not sheep.

Red tongue draping the dog's jaw,
burrs in his belly hair,
ear tuned to his slouching master,
who chugs a Coke, whistles an order.

Overhead scent of bay laurel,
wet clay on the trail,
jerking ankle from tibia, femur from pelvis.
Who gets the drumstick:
me or this greasy, bottomless substrate?

The brain tires of hounding its thoughts,
marshalling them across the vast and oozy
floodplain of the mind
toward some endgame, stop game, home.

Lucky dog running on pure trust
for a guy who leans on a truck,
squinting into puffy clouds.

In this sometime feast of sunlight,
stuff yourselves and take your fill.
A long time gone, as every other herder
of thoughts has sung.

Gibbous moon tonight,

Regulus to the East in Leo,
white-edged, blue at the center.
Hotter than the sun,
it won't outlive. Burning as we speak.

MOON OVER ZABRISKIE

IV

Sense of Direction

From the ridge the lake's a granite lip,
tongue of water, nearly a mirage.
Farthest north, a compass needle
would careen in confused circles.

In the forest the ground smells of drying out,
dampness rising collides
with the heat, yields.

Nothing's bloomed except in possibility,
closed flowers, before color, before form:
owl clover, blue larkspur, penstemon,
the ferns are curled monkey paws.

What Delacroix meant when he said,
One never paints violently enough.

The day, the year half over, I want a prize,
a squirrel jawbone, snakeskin,
or oriole feather.
Something to ease the descent.

Here are puffball mushrooms,
white spheres, patterned brains of creatures
spawned underground, released too soon,
waiting for their bodies to grow,
afterlife in reverse.

Silver Lake Rituals

Tethered by a flexible leash
to her backroom machine, Mona's
gone on oxygen, but she can sell
hooks, live worms, and lead sinkers.
There's dust on the box of cookies
I didn't buy last year, the year before.
Her silver canister of air (*my ethereal
angel, or is that redundant?* she asks)
glides by on silver tires; she says
this week the fish are so full
of themselves, they'll jump down
your throat. The stars come out
in little breaths. Some angel,
ethereal or not, gives Mona a good
night's rest. Her generator hums
off-key all night, while trucks
haul Nevada down to the valley—
sun-cured hay and just-cut timber.
Whips of scent and green sprigs flung
out in passing. The boats *tlock-tlock*
against the pier, impatient for dawn.
Load them down with human weight,
crank up those little engines and go.

Blue Jay Morning

A dark flit of cobalt outside my window,
the bird comes to tell me what for
and then some, daring me to rise to bait.
No heft today,

so toss me back into the water. Into sleep,
my ruffle-top ruffian, I'll rather be,
but I'll slide into your day. Today, in '37,
Amelia Earhart slipped through,

her blue line tangled. Out of a blue sky,
she's still slipping through
July, which is a clamor of suntan,
good teeth, and "hellos" down the mountain.

The wind roughs up the lake,
chasing heat back down the valley;
the lake surface blazes, blinding
as a snowfield or a shield's veneer

or the world's thin membrane. The bird
returns to dive my eyes
and my tangled hair for nest fodder.
Soon enough, wise guy, but not today.

Found feathers a diminished blue—
they need the body heated by flight
to keep the hue, as if fingertip struck
from a match as glimpsed

at the margin of sight on this bird,
this eyelash of Heaven, aniline blue,
sliding down morning's nicked jawline.

Borrego Springs

Openmouthed to a stranger
at a roadside fruit stand who is dripping
honey on my tongue from a plastic spoon,

I know that light is an amateur's try by the sun
at Impressionism's crafty work,
imposing upon the desert at noon

this blanched-out, transient unity,
reducing the hour to Inferno's sizzle and fry.
In the Scissor light, Rock heat—you're Paper,
blank and moodless, easily crumpled.

At midday the desert's inner strangeness
has vanished, dissolved in platinum Jean Harlow air.

The man tenders his swarm of bees
in the grapefruit orchard. *A mouthful of paradise,
see for yourself. That's the beauty of a drought year,
there's nothing ripe enough to decay.*

In the gap between what's seen around us and the void,
there's one small hinge. *Keep it shiny, keep it oiled.*
At evening the shadows slip back into town,
unpack their bags, yawn, and stretch out,

restoring to people and palm trees, to the yellow school bus
and spotted roadside dogs, our shape and heft.
Then the wind, too, blows back
from the Salton Sea, that old hair-lasher, skin-flayer.
Midair, the bluebirds scramble for purchase.

If The Desert Acts Familiar, Push Back

Leave a white hair, a fingernail sliver,
or a button off your blue shirt,
wrapped in mallow leaf

and laced with a mesquite thorn.
Bury it for 10 years or 20,
then come here looking, if we're living,
but remember where to dig.

The sand dunes are displaying, revising,
and erasing our portraits, whether traces
of animal, human, or the South wind;
we are all bystanders, transient and welcome.

At evening the birds in a flock
with urgent business on Earth
bend sharp left and sharp right.
Under the nearly full moon,

a thin tatting of cloud cover,
Orion on his side over Zabriskie Point,
kicking his sheets off,
tugs them back up to his shoulders.

Someone tell me, please,
what's he dreaming tonight?

The Yellow Sand Road

It winds around to the old hotel—
Frank Morgan slept here.
Scarecrow? No, he played the Wizard,
that floating head, that imposter prince,

that one-time honorary mayor of Borrego Springs,
when this hotel served *young roast
of tom turkey breast for three bucks,*
invited ladies *to wear strapless,*

invited all, tour the naval bombing zone,
take your camera.
Eisenhower, with his too-many teeth,
and Mamie waving.

Warning signs abound today for mountain lion,
with trailside debates whether best
to beat pans and holler
or curl in the dust and play dead.

I'd play dead and prefer the Scarecrow.
Chaff for brains and nearly lifelike
with a name, clothes, job to do:
cast a shadow, rustle, and smile.

Behind the hotel sat 65 cabanas,
the room and bath, sleeps four,
suburbanlike, desert demidreams.
Lay down one pink tile, another pink, now try aqua—
that's what some guy did years ago to leave his mark,
no two shower floors the same.

Now there's nothing left but one Palo Verde
quivering with bluebirds,
the gleam of broken mosaic on concrete pads
and a dozen walls with paint so blistered,
bubbled, and tormented by heat,
you'd think that hearts had broken here.
Someday I'll quit stalking the dawn

with a notebook and a camera,
scouring nostalgia's wreckage and hoping
for a mountain lion, but not today.

There's pink tile to pocket
and a cholla cactus in citrine bloom.

Palm Canyon

Four bighorn sheep in a bachelor herd,
camouflaged as sandstone,
schist, chuparosa, and desert lavender,
step out from the beige, out of near mirage,

choppy-breathed and their teeth to the leaves
of the mesquite bush, hooves clicking
through the wash, then
they melt back, gone through the smoke trees.

Can't help thinking about Abraham
with Isaac, that ram with his horns
tangled in thicket, his neck looped back

beneath the gleaming blade. Abraham busy
heeding the voice of *Now do this,
Now do that,* shifts his eyes from the gaze
of his son, of the ram, but now

the palm trees at noon sway as they're meant to,
carving the air space. They are

shallow-rooted surface feeders; it's amazing what little
holds them in place. There was a call
from ward 14 E and his old voice
telling me, *They think I hear voices, they've
locked me, so get me out; you'll come for me,*

won't you? And I didn't. Get him out
from there. These pieces of memory
held, fluttering—his gray eyes,
his long fingers flat-picking
a 12-string. Hope's a flat rock

we fling into next year
and the year after, saying:
Find your mark, we'll catch up with you.

Gold Canyon

You can tell it wants a flash-flood,
the shape of its face altered
by a storm from distant mountains.

At the quarter slots, Vegas airport,
I kept a three-dollar limit.
Deposit, click, repeat, sevens slowing down,
eyeing one another. It's a date
of bright flashing, a rush of loud, cold silver.

Once, when I couldn't make rent,
when I was a bad waitress, a failed school bus driver,
I'd have loved this then.

Can't resist plunging in up to my wrists,
how it pours over me, between my fingers,
all my betrayals, my greeds. People gather,

a man asking, *Can I touch you? For good luck?*
Not for my charms. Cash cow—I am regal,
cheap, exotic, and full of despair.
If they only knew this, these watchers, would they take on
my sin?

At Zabriskie Point
the tight creek beds, the arms of yellow land
try to lace fingers across the chasm.

The late light probes and strokes.
The striated hills give up
and turn over in the shade.

There's gravel underfoot into the canyon,
the alluvial wash fanning out,
somewhere mythic washerwomen
once scrubbed their linens.
Anna was, Plurabelle's to be.

The eye tires of too much beauty.
At four the light's high carat, it's at full saturation.
Then it thins, it alloys with tin, silver, copper,
drops to 14, 12 carats of affordable light.

Half this lived life later, I come back,
same landscape as before, same folds of hills,
still wanting to enter each canyon,
climb through as if it were a body.

Moon Over Zabriskie

It's the Parkinson's, he says, counting out change,
a young guy selling me a 50-cent lighter.
Violent shakes up to his elbows
but so careful at his fingertips,
he must be able to hear through them.

From the Death Valley Saloon next door,
there's Patsy, scratchy on the jukebox—
tears come down like falling rain—
she wants a floor to walk, a name to call.

The tall drunk behind me in line, saying,
Lady, your lighter's kidproof, there's a hidden button.
Careful with words, he sets each one down—
a man testing his weight across the ice.

East of here, not much to see
of the Nevada test sight, you'd have to imagine
or remember—the obscure sign about danger,
rusted out, grown over—the blasted-pummeled land.

Two men with their four shaky hands
teach me how to free the fire
of my blue plastic lighter.
Could be I've made their night.

The drunk so young and skinny,
you know he's bought the same lighter,
wrestled its secret, spares me the pain.

Me with my one lousy glass of white,
one smoke per night, he's the pro at dissolution,
brief glance at his eyes—
a cliff with a long way down.
His hands are petals.

Too much finagling, not enough staring
into the night. This desert used to intimidate,
I'd like that fear back now while it can be used,
fear of being peeled back, skinned clean.

Furnace Creek Breakdown

Creosote plant can explode, they say,
into flames but usually doesn't.
The sardine-tin lid of the sky peels back,
and birds fly one by one to Heaven.

The Badwater salt flats crackle.
You walk out and halt
and stare into the glaring,

not the *gloaming*, which is familial,
which is where you stare into green
and think of what's lost.

No, not this place,
which makes you remember being alive,
not the build up or nor the tumble down.

Gold Canyon twists you into it.
You're a lock of hair in its fingers,
the walls steep red and copper,

pulling you into brilliance
and blindness. Into this fire
where, for the moment,
I am gladly diminished.
How to tell rock from mineral,
The ranger saying,
It's a matter of hardness,
cleavage and fracture.

Arrested in flight, we catchers of sunlight,
with pickleweed, pupfish,
and gleaming thorns of mesquite,
our purple shadows crossing the salt flat.

Titus Canyon

Sand is bigger than dust, smaller than pebbles,
all of them rub one another
in and out of being,
sand dunes at sunset are desert saints,
peeling spirit from body,

peeling six crows from the picnic table,
one leftover pizza. A coyote who stalks,
feints, waits, plump and easy—
his patience, their pride.

Wanting to enter the desert. Below the skin.
Come out altered.
Donatello's *Magdalena* carved in wood,
head of hair from crown to foot sole,
with huge eyes staring, windows to somewhere.

Shooting star over the Panamint mountains
air-lifting a soul out of life—
that's what my father believed. Noiseless flight
in and out of being. Flaring
on your retina, faint traces etched in.

Press lightly on the membrane of time,
translucent down to the man
I brought here once. Little boiled meal
at Wild Rose Canyon,
shivering in crummy sleeping bags.
How happy we thought we were.
Love me forever—will you, won't you?
A life of small and great pleasures.
From this distance they seem the same.
Black road south to Badwater,
aluminum light, alluvial spillage,
salt flats fluorescent at night.

Autumn Ballad

The moon in its last quarter,
and over Orion's right shoulder,
here's red-tinged Betelgeuse
shouldering up above the horizon.
Some nights, when the mind splinters

and flies off into slivers—
would that each fragment would travel
to lovely places and slink home with photos,

bring me stories, some news of the world
that I could jagged-stitch and rough-nail
into something entirely new.

You, Orion, up there,
with your dagger and dogs,
banished for careless love,
silly boy to get caught,
spare a word or two tonight,
any spurious paraphrase will do.

Sun don't shine, as my father said,
on the same dog every day,
which is why the other song that he sang,

stumbling home late from a bad card game, was
*Tie a shoe, button your shirt, cry together
till catfish gleam, come June, in the lowland stream.*
In one choice miracle St. Francis rids a woman
in a blue dress of what ails her,
which the painter renders
as a delicate, winged devil
flitting out of her through her slackened mouth.

At which point we viewers demand to know
whether divine grace arrived, all set
to set up house in the vacuum, or if this woman,

scrawny and ravaged, divested of her ailment,
pined away in a beige existence
for all the awful little things she was made
to think and say.
How harmless they may seem now.

Late Night Stroll in the Valley

Full moon lying sideways
over the Funeral Mountains,
her face big-eyed,
her mouth a small *O*,

saying, *Oh*, in surprise,
Medusa seeing herself
and him in the mirror.
The sword is falling.

She didn't know
that he'd have green eyes,
that he'd be young
and lyrical. He neither

hates nor fears her.
This would take years
to digest, and she
hasn't the years.

That sword
is still falling.
She is neither shocked
nor resistant tonight,

just stunned.
It's after dinner,
nearly bedtime.
She was in full swing.
And weren't we all.

Photo: Eliot Khuner

Helen Wickes was raised on a horse farm in south-eastern Pennsylvania. She attended Vassar College. She now lives in Oakland, California, and worked for many years as a psychotherapist. She received an MFA from the Bennington Writing Seminars. Her first book of poems, *In Search of Landscape*, was published in 2007 by Sixteen Rivers Press. Glass Lyre Press published *Dowser's Apprentice* in 2014, and in 2015, Sixteen Rivers Press will publish *The World as You Left It*.

GLASS LYRE PRESS, LLC
"Exceptional works to replenish the spirit"

Poetry collections
Poetry chapbooks
Select short & flash fiction
Occasional anthologies

Glass Lyre Press is a small independent literary press interested in work which is technically accomplished and distinctive in style, as well as fresh in its approach and treatment. Glass Lyre seeks writers of diverse backgrounds who display mastery over the many areas of contemporary literature: writers with a powerful and dynamic aesthetic, and ability to stir the imagination and engage the emotions and intellect of a wide audience of readers.

The Glass Lyre vision is to connect the world through language and art. We hope to expand the scope of poetry and short fiction for the general reader through exceptionally well-written books, which call forth our deepest emotions and thoughts, delight our senses, challenge our minds, and provide clarity, resonance and insight.

www.GlassLyrePress.com

www.ingramcontent.com/pod-product-compliance
Lightning Source LLC
Chambersburg PA
CBHW020700300426
44112CB00007B/465